EARTH'S WATER

Say Hello to H2O

by Ellen Lawrence

Consultant:

Howard Perlman, Hydrologist

BEARPORT
PUBLISHING

New York, New York

Credits

Cover, © Rita Kochmarjova/Shutterstock; 4, © elwynn/Shutterstock; 5, © Johan Swanepoel/Shutterstock; 6, © Ruby Tuesday Books, © Lightspring/Shutterstock, and © Rashevskyi Viacheslav/Shutterstock; 7, © Tischenko Irina/Shutterstock; 8, © Fuse/Thinkstock; 8B, © photopeerayut/Shutterstock; 9TL, © Vaclav Volrab /Shutterstock; 9TR, © yanikap/Shutterstock; 9BL, © Pi-Lens/Shutterstock; 9BR, © Soru Epotok /Shutterstock; 10, © SJ Travel Photo and Video/Shutterstock; 11, © Vadim Petrakov/Shutterstock; 12, © Ruby Tuesday Books and © Lightspring/Shutterstock; 13, © Aggie 11/Shutterstock; 14, © Colette3/Shutterstock; 15, © Getty Images/Thinkstock; 16, © James Stevenson/Getty Images; 17, © Derek Middleton/FLPA; 18TL, © SJ Travel Photo and Video/Shutterstock; 18TR, © Steve Byland/Shutterstock; 18B, © Aspen Photo/Shutterstock; 19, © donfiore/Shutterstock; 20, © Ingram Publishing/Thinkstock; 21, © Vasiliy Koval/Shutterstock; 22, © Ruby Tuesday Books; 23TL, © photopeerayut/Shutterstock; 23TC, © Phil Lenoir/Shutterstock; 23TR, © Lightspring/Shutterstock; 23BL, © Filipe B. Varela/Shutterstock; 23BC, © Filipe B. Varela/Shutterstock; 23BR, © Vaclav Volrab/Shutterstock.

Publisher: Kenn Goin
Editor: Jessica Rudolph
Creative Director: Spencer Brinker
Design: Emma Randall
Photo Researcher: Ruby Tuesday Books Ltd

Library of Congress Cataloging-in-Publication Data

Names: Lawrence, Ellen, 1967– author.
Title: Say hello to H2O / by Ellen Lawrence.
Other titles: Say hello to water
Description: New York, New York : Bearport Publishing, [2016] | Series: Drip, drip, drop: Earth's water | Audience: Ages 6–10. | Includes bibliographical references and index.
Identifiers: LCCN 2015040333 (print) | LCCN 2015042603 (ebook) | ISBN 9781943553211 (library binding) | ISBN 9781943553556 (ebook)
Subjects: LCSH: Water—Juvenile literature. | Hydrology—Juvenile literature.
Classification: LCC GB662.3 .L3935 2016 (print) | LCC GB662.3 (ebook) | DDC 553.7—dc23
LC record available at http://lccn.loc.gov/2015040333

For more information, write to Bearport Publishing Company, Inc., 45 West 21st Street, Suite 3B, New York, New York 10010. Printed in the United States of America.

10 9 8 7 6 5 4 3 2 1

Contents

Pouring, Splashing, Flowing Water!

Water is a part of our everyday lives.

When you turn on a faucet, water pours out.

During a storm, rainwater trickles onto the ground.

Water has no color, smell, or taste, and yet it's amazing stuff.

So what exactly is water, and why is it so special?

What words can you use to describe water? Make a list in a notebook.

One of the **properties** of liquid water is that it has no shape. Like all liquids, water takes the shape of whatever container it's in—from a bottle to an elephant's trunk!

Why Is Water Called H$_2$O?

Everything, including water, is made of tiny parts called atoms.

When atoms join together, they form a **molecule**.

A molecule of water is made of two hydrogen (H) atoms and one oxygen (O) atom.

This is why water is called H$_2$O.

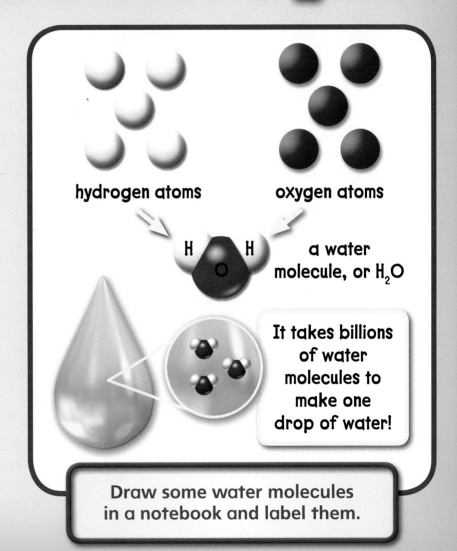

hydrogen atoms

oxygen atoms

a water molecule, or H$_2$O

It takes billions of water molecules to make one drop of water!

Draw some water molecules in a notebook and label them.

There's oxygen
in both air and water.
People breathe in oxygen
from the air with their lungs.
How do fish breathe?
They use body parts called
gills to take in oxygen
from water.

7

Sticky Water

Another property of water is that it appears to be sticky.

When raindrops trickle down a window, they seem to cling, or stick, to the glass.

If two drops touch, they join together, forming a bigger drop.

This happens because water molecules are **attracted** to each other and to other surfaces.

two or more drops forming a large drop

When water molecules stick to each other, it's called cohesion (koh-HEE-zhuhn). When water sticks to another surface, it's called adhesion (ad-HEE-zhuhn).

In a notebook, describe the water in these four pictures using the words *cohesion* and *adhesion*.
(An example is given on page 24.)

9

Holding It Together

Look closely at a drop of water.

It looks as if an outer layer is holding the water together.

All the water molecules in the drop are sticking together because of cohesion.

However, the water molecules on the outside of the drop are sticking together even more tightly.

This property is called surface tension.

pond skaters
walking on water

Some insects,
such as pond skaters,
can move across a pond
or lake without breaking the
outer layer of the water. This
is due to surface tension and
because the insects are very
light and have specially
shaped legs.

Water on the Move

The stickiness of water helps it move.

If you dip the corner of a paper towel into water, the water climbs up the towel!

This happens because water molecules stick to the towel and then start to move upward.

Other molecules then cling to the first ones and are pulled up the towel.

This is called capillary action.

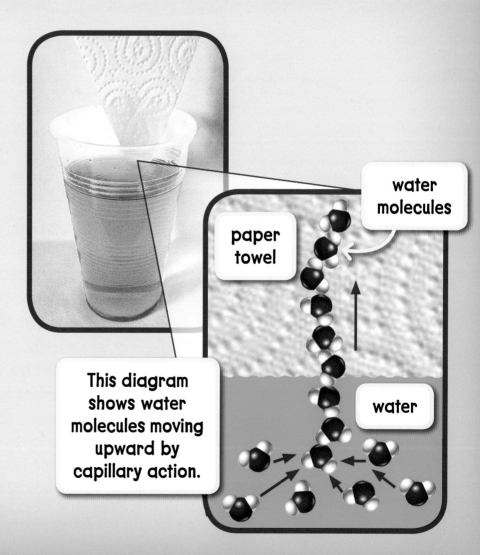

water molecules

paper towel

water

This diagram shows water molecules moving upward by capillary action.

roots

Capillary action is very important to plants. Why? A plant takes in water from soil through its roots. Then capillary action causes the water to climb up the plant's roots, stem, and leaves.

13

Where Did It Go?

If you stir a spoonful of sugar into water, the sugar disappears. Why?

Sugar and many other substances **dissolve** in water.

This property of water helps plants survive.

To grow and be healthy, plants need **nutrients** that are in soil.

Nutrients dissolve in water in the soil, and then plants take the nutrient-rich water in through their roots.

Ocean water has lots of salt dissolved in it. You can't see the salt, but you can taste it. In fact, 1 pint (473 ml) of seawater contains about 1 teaspoon (5 ml) of salt.

From a Liquid to a Solid

Water drips, trickles, splashes, and flows.

When the temperature drops to 32°F (0°C), however, it turns from a liquid into solid ice.

As water freezes, it expands, so ice takes up more space than liquid water.

When a plastic bottle of water is put in a freezer, the ice that forms may even crack the bottle!

a cracked bottle filled with ice

When you drop ice cubes into water, do they sink or float? Water is heavier than ice, so ice always floats. That's why when a lake freezes, the layer of ice is on top and the liquid water is underneath.

an otter walking on a frozen lake

Water can be a liquid and a solid. It also has a third state. What do you think it is?

Water in the Air

Water has three states—liquid, solid, and a gas called water vapor.

Liquid water turns into a gas when it is heated.

When the sun's heat warms up a puddle, some of the water disappears.

It **evaporates** and becomes water vapor in the air.

You can't see water vapor, but it's floating all around you!

liquid

solid

water vapor in the air

When water vapor cools, it turns back into liquid water. You can see this on a cold metal can. When water vapor touches the cold metal, it changes into water drops on the can.

drops of liquid water

H₂O Is All Around

Water is everywhere—in the air, under the ground, inside plants, and even in you.

In fact, your body is about 60 percent water.

So say hello to wonderful H_2O.

We may not always notice it, but it's all around, and it's amazing stuff!

Plants contain lots of water, and so do foods that come from plants. A crunchy apple or carrot is about 85 percent water. A juicy tomato or watermelon is more than 90 percent water!

21

Science Lab

Water drops stick together because of cohesion. You can see cohesion in action in this fun investigation.

How Many Water Drops Will Fit on a Penny?

You will need:
- A penny
- Water
- An eyedropper
- A notebook and a pencil

1. Place a penny on a table or countertop.

2. Collect some water in the eyedropper and squeeze one drop of water onto the penny.

3. Now add a second drop of water to the penny.

   What are the drops doing?

   How many more drops do you think will fit on the penny?

   Write your prediction in your notebook.

4. Continue to add water drops to the penny. Record the number of drops in your notebook using tally marks. Keep adding drops until the water spills off the penny.

   Did the number of drops match your prediction?

one drop

several drops

Number of Water Drops:

⊮⊮⊮⊮ ⊮⊮⊮⊮

⊮⊮⊮⊮ |||

Science Words

attracted (uh-TRAK-tihd) pulled toward another object or substance

dissolve (dih-ZAWLV) to break down substances in a liquid into smaller parts

evaporates (i-VAP-uh-rayts) turns from a liquid into a gas

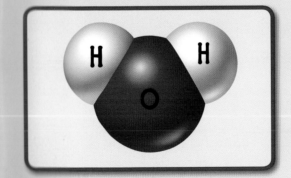

molecule (MAHL-uh-kyool) two or more atoms joined together

nutrients (NOO-tree-uhnts) substances needed by plants to grow and stay healthy

properties (PRAH-pur-teez) the special qualities of something that make it what it is

Index

Read More

Lawrence, Ellen. *Water (FUN-damental Experiments).* New York: Bearport (2013).

Rosinsky, Natalie M. *Water: Up, Down, and All Around.* Mankato, MN: Picture Window Books (2003).

Salas, Laura Purdie. *Water Can Be ... (Millbrook Picture Books).* Minneapolis, MN: Lerner (2014).

Learn More Online

To learn more about the properties of water, visit
www.bearportpublishing.com/DripDripDrop

About the Author

Ellen Lawrence lives in the United Kingdom. Her favorite books to write are those about nature and animals. In fact, the first book Ellen bought for herself, when she was six years old, was the story of a gorilla named Patty Cake that was born in New York's Central Park Zoo.

Answer for Page 9

The water drops clinging to the plants, the ladybug, and the spiderweb are examples of adhesion. The larger water drops are examples of cohesion, since they are made from many small drops that stuck together.